Faith Building

A "How To" Guide for Designing and Building New and Expanded Ministry Facilities.

The design and construction of a facility to be utilized in a ministry must start with prayer, followed by careful planning. A congregation's dreams are realized when a well-planned process of commitment and communication is executed properly.

By

Companies

Published by D.E.M. Publishing
A Division of COMPASS Consultants Corporation
ramckenzie.compass@gmail.com

Faith Building

A "How To" Guide for Designing and Building New and Expanded Ministry Facilities.

All Rights Reserved. Copyright© 2014

ISBN: 978-0-578-09995-8
Printed in the United States of America
10 9 8 7 6 5 4 3 2 1
First Edition

2014

This book is about the process of planning, facility design and construction for effective faith based ministry. It will provide an inside perspective on seven key areas of facility design and construction to guide a church and its ministry leaders and building teams. If followed in sequence, this book will assist your team as you seek to find direction in which the vision of your ministry can become a reality. Purposeful, well designed religious facilities contribute to the environment of faith building. This guidebook is meant to provide proven real life useful information to help all of those involved with ministry planning, design and construction of their new facilities.

Dedication

To Christian Leaders, Building and Planning Teams
who Seek Knowledge, Guidance and Wisdom
to Lead People to Christ.

PBS Church Visioning Group
Dale Reiser

*Thank you to Ross, Naomi, Chad, Brad, Bryan,
Eric, Paula, Erik and Karin*

Table of Contents

Pastor Greg Eilders
Peoples Church

It became obvious it was time to build. We had survived, and even thrived as "a church in the wilderness," we called it, holding services in the ballroom of a local hotel for the previous 5 years. "Set up, take down, set up, take down," had been our weekly routine. However, we were also feeling the effects of not being able to function ideally as a growing church to disciple and train beyond Sunday mornings. It was time!

Early on, the leadership of the church had settled upon design/ build, rather than take on the weight and stress of a new building project ourselves. We did not want to allow ourselves to be side-tracked from the church growth we were seeing, but where to go and how to proceed?

Our assumption was that there were probably many church-design builders, as well as, independent contractors and builders involved in the construction industry, that could build a church. Our priorities were to focus on "integrity" and "character" of this vital relationship. Could we trust them? The ability of those we would partner with had to be able to "capture our vision" and take that vision and put pen to paper. Above all, though, we desired a relationship we could trust.

Not only were we novices, we were skeptical. However, the approach of PBS, who became the design/build team we contracted with, immediately alleviated our apprehensions. They listened to our *building team* as each expressed the dreams and vision of this future church building. The aura our building team desired to create was one of warmth in a non-threatening, non-intimidating environment so often associated with churches, and we desired that people would experience that as soon as they walked through the doors.

This, we felt, would enhance the development of the community atmosphere we desired to create. Not only did PBS capture that, but they exceeded our expectations. An inviting fireplace (we're in the north), and a coffee shop with bistro tables and chairs would catch the eye of first-time guests as they entered. PBS ultimately *captured that vision*, as well as, master-planned a church design that included infrastructure for the next phase of 3 phases.

Perhaps the greatest aspect with PBS was the relationship that began with them. From that first informal get-together, to the completion of the 1st phase, it continues as an on-going relationship. They are not only integral partners, but they are also *friends*.

A relationship was forged that went beyond bricks and mortar, something far more intrinsic than that. They became friends, and that does not always happen with undertakings as magnanimous as a church construction project!

Loyalty is a virtue. But, it must be earned. PBS understood that!

"PBS was able to capture the vision we had as a church. They came through for us and we have begun our second building phase with them."

Greg Eilders, Pastor
Peoples Church

Pastor Dennis Papp
SouthField Church

***Walking into Channahon Junior High School on a Sunday
morning***, one would conclude that SouthField Church is a church
plant, like so many inhabiting the schools of our communities.
In reality, we are one of the oldest existing churches in the Joliet
area. SouthField was planted by a group of Swedish immigrants in
1881 as the First Swedish Baptist Church.

In the early 2000's, our church experienced a burst of growth unlike
any in our history. Attendance doubled and then nearly doubled
again. Growth was exciting, but our building was designed for a
much smaller church and had little potential for expansion.

In 2004 we purchased 14 acres about 15 minutes south of our
location of over forty years. Enthusiasm was high as we set out
on this exciting venture. We hired an architect and designed an
ambitious facility.

To make the move possible, we needed to sell our building and move
into an interim facility. We found an ideal location at Channahon
Junior High. After a long season of prayer and preparation, we
placed our building on the market and set the moving date—
September 2008.

Two things happened during that season that would mark our
journey for the next few years. Weeks before moving, the architect
came back with an estimate over double what we requested and
knew we could afford. We also moved within days of what we
now know to be the start of the worst financial crisis since the
Depression.

The strong momentum we felt in the summer of 2008 left our sails
quickly. By winter, our leadership team realized that our wilderness

experience would likely last longer than we had hoped. By 2012, we started to wonder aloud about our future. Attendance was dwindling. Momentum was flat. Our dreams of a building were locked away in a metal cabinet in a storage facility. We knew we needed to do something, but the something we needed seemed absolutely unattainable.

I contacted PBS and asked a simple question, "What do you think we can build with what we have?" Our property was paid in full and we had a decent start on a building fund. From the first meeting, PBS expressed hope.

Hope. I have to admit, I had not felt hope for a long time. Hope had been beaten out of me one painful disappointment at a time. I was so hopeless that I had stopped even looking at the property when I drove by. I would turn my head. The pain of dreaming was too harsh.

I was skeptical. I had heard *hope* from our first designer. This time, we needed more than just wishful thinking. I was adamant. We did not need another set of unbuildable plans to add to our expensive cabinet of unbuildable buildings.

PBS got to work and designed a facility that met our needs and was within our budget. For the first time in years, there was a ripple of momentum in our sails. A slight breeze of hope was beginning to blow. In July 2013, we voted unanimously to move ahead. Last April, dirt began to move and a structure started to emerge from the ground under PBS' project management leadership.

The journey with PBS has been nothing but positive. They are true to their word, professional in every sense of the word and they listen, which is so rare these days. In our case, they are doing more than just building a facility. They've restored our ability to dream—to hope.

Almost every night I head to the property to take pictures. Often my sight is blurred with tears, not only because our church will soon have a home, but also because we are daring to dream again. We have PBS to thank for both.

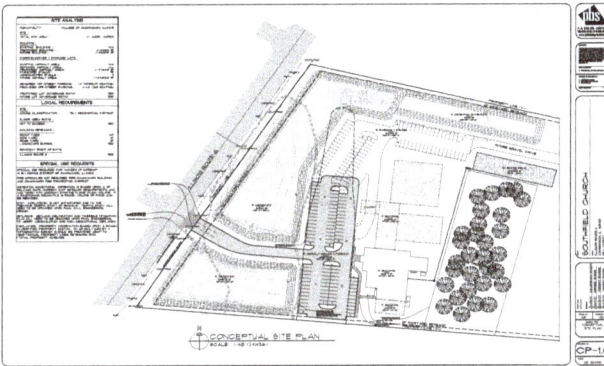

I contacted PBS and asked a simple question, "What do you think we can build with what we have?" Our property was paid in full and we had a decent start on a building fund. From the first meeting, PBS expressed hope.

Dennis Papp, Pastor
SouthField Church

Foreword

The purpose of this book is to provide a platform for better understanding the building process. It does so by separating that process into seven key parts and then linking them with the wisdom and blessing of experience.

Following are some of the common statements churches make when they realize their current situation is not meeting their needs:

- *We need to expand.*
- *We need to relocate to a larger site.*
- *Our present facility is outdated; we need to renovate to make our building more suitable for our current needs.*

That's how it starts – by God preparing the hearts of church members to recognize a need. That need may be in the form of community outreach, internal expansion of programs to facilitate spiritual growth within the membership or establishing special support programs for those in need.

In a very tangible manner, the First Step in Faith Building is realizing there is a *reason* for building. Since ministry boards do not build every day, there will normally be more questions than answers in the beginning - questions like:

- *How do we do this?*
- *What do we build?*
- *How do we pay for it?*

An Exciting Journey
This book is offered as a guide for those in your church who have accepted the responsibility of leading the journey of designing and building your new facility. They are given the responsibility and challenge of making the right decisions to move your new building or expansion project forward.

All buildings depend upon a solid foundation; likewise, this book will provide a solid foundation for facility planning, design and construction. Whether you are considering a new building on a green site, a renovation, or repurposing an existing space, this book will be a catalyst in getting the process started in a thoughtful, step by step method.

The basis for making a difference in ministry planning, design and construction is easy.

Imagine your dream,
make your dream part of your thinking,
make it happen.

The thoughts and concepts in this book will help you with all three of these steps. It is more than a guide as it will provide you with a way of thinking about your project. As has been demonstrated countless times, careful planning, wrapped in prayer, is an platform for God to allow our dreams to become reality.

Introduction

The construction of a building is much like a jigsaw puzzle. The pieces are designed to fit together in only one way and some pieces must be put in place before others. Although the methods used in putting a jigsaw puzzle together can vary, the basic requirements of the construction of a building cannot.

First comes a solid foundation, next comes the framework that defines the walls and roof, then the closing in of those walls and roof, and finally the internal finishing of the space. Of course, this is an over-simplification of the whole process. Each of these steps involves numerous jobs that must be coordinated and put together in proper sequence... just like the jigsaw puzzle. This book outlines Seven Key Steps involved in putting the *puzzle pieces* of a construction project together to the satisfaction of all involved.

1. *Construction Delivery*
2. *The PBS 5-Step Delivery Process*
3. *Needs and Wants of Ministry Design*
4. *Prayer/Planning*
5. *Financial*
6. *Closeout*
7. *Ministry During Construction*

Sample interior rendering as presented to the-
customer during PBS design process.

During a guest preaching assignment and just before accepting the Teaching Pastor position at West Ridge Community Church Gordon Venturella stated: "For the past 14 years or so, I have traveled all over this country and have been in a lot of church buildings...and this is the best church facility I've ever been in, period."

Gordon Venturella
Teaching Pastor West Ridge Community Church

PROVERBS 3:5-6

Trust in the lord with all your heart, and lean not on
your own understanding; in all your ways submit to him,
and he will make your paths straight.

CHAPTER 1
Construction Delivery

IN THE BEGINNING, the most frequently asked question by
building and leadership teams tasked with building a project, is:
How do we start the process?

Construction delivery is a subject that most people struggle to
understand. This stands to reason as most people are not involved in
designing or constructing buildings. This is a logical place to begin
our discussion with church leaders and building teams as they
contemplate the multiple tasks involved in building a new facility
or expanding an existing one.

Certainly there are steps that must be taken before the delivery
process starts, such as planning and design, but a full understanding
of the *construction delivery* methods is vital when making the
decision of which method to use.

> *"While a design/build firm, PBS has completed
> successful projects under all methods of construction
> delivery. Understanding the differences in
> construction delivery will help in the overall project,
> no matter what method is utilized."*

The construction industry has always sought methods and processes
to provide better service in delivering the project to the owner.
Start by determining the most appropriate delivery method for
your particular situation, or leadership team, then consult with

your design and construction team to fully understand how it will work best for your ministry.

The purpose in discussing these three construction delivery methods, is to understand how these services differ from each other and how they affect the owner.

Three basic delivery systems will be discussed.
- *Traditional Delivery—Design-Bid-Build*
- *Construction Management, or CM*
- *Design/Build*

The three delivery methods are defined as follows:

Traditional Delivery - Design-Bid-Build

Under this method, the owner contracts with an architect, who designs the project and prepares bidding documents, which eventually leads to the selection of the general contractor. The criteria for selection is generally based upon a lump sum price.

Under this model the architect receives direction from the church/school (ministry), a wish list if you will, on the design. It isn't until later, as mentioned above, when a design is complete that actual project costs are determined. This comes after bids are sought based upon the completed design.

Presuming that the costs provided are deemed *affordable*, the lowest qualified bidder is usually awarded the project through another separate contract. Should the bidding process show that the costs are not affordable or over the anticipated budget, as is often the case, the design process starts over again to modify the design. Then the project again goes through the bidding process seeking a contract value affordable to the church. The architect, or another separate entity, under yet another separate contract, observes the construction and administration of the contracts. This usually entails a *closed book* approach, meaning the price of the subcontracts is not necessarily disclosed as this method is a lump sum method.

Construction Management

A Construction Manager, or CM, as an agent of the owner, builds the project from construction documents prepared by an architect. The CM is compensated based upon a fixed fee or percentage of construction costs. When structured properly, the CM usually enters the project early-on and provides value engineering, budget and schedule input. The subcontracts are still competitively bid, but there are no mark-ups of the subcontracts from the CM to the owner. The project is *open book*, as all numbers are know to the owner. Generally in this arrangement the owner assumes all responsibility for the design and engineering documents.

Design/Build

To start, in an era long ago, when castles and cathedrals were being built, the projects sometimes lasted for years – sometimes as witnessed in scripture, they were life-long projects for the King. These projects came under the auspices of one person, the *master builder*, who designed and built the castle, or cathedral.

This is important to mention because that *master builder* system is still with us today in the form of design/build. As will be explained, this system stands out as a seamless stress relieving method. The design/build method will provide ministries the ability to have as little or as much input as is desired at all stages of the project without detracting from day to day ministry responsibilities.

Design and construction services are packaged under one contract, as a single source of project delivery for all design and construction services. Similar to CM, the project remains an open book throughout the project. Under this method however, the design/build firm assumes one hundred percent responsibility.

21

The Various Delivery Methods Explained

Traditional Delivery (Design-Bid-Build)

This is the *traditional* method by which construction services have been delivered. The architect participates in the pre-design phases, prepares schematic drawings and the final design and construction documents, secures the building permit, *then* bids out the work based upon the owner's input. *Then*, the lowest qualified general contractor is selected.

This is also referred to as hard-bid and is touted by many, often including attorneys, as the only way that the lowest possible price can be obtained due to the competitive bidding. This is false, because there is competitive bidding in all the delivery methods. This, unfortunately, can also often result in a contract being awarded to an unqualified general contractor *simply on the basis of price.*

One significant concern with this delivery method is that in many instances it can create adversarial relationships between the architect, engineers, contractor and the owner/ministry. For example, if a low bid contractor determines there are inconsistencies in the design he will go to the architect and state that the drawings are not clear on a particular item, thereby creating a change order to the church. This results in not only increased costs but also lost time in what is often a sensitive project schedule. Challenges mount as parties involved often cast doubt on each other's ability in the eyes of the owner.

The sad truth is that there are hard-bid contractors that deliberately create adversarial relationships so they can challenge the architect and the subcontractor team, thereby creating situations where they can add profit by taking advantage of the situation. It is difficult to determine who these contractors might be and it can be exasperating. When a contractor comes in with an attractive low bid, often a church will learn later that he has little or no experience in building church or ministry related buildings. The temptation however is to use that contractor to get the *best price* out of an unintentional motive to be good stewards of the ministry dollars. By comparison, it is important to note here that both the CM and design/build delivery system have built in safe guards to avoid this possibility. This is why the pre-qualification of the bidders by the owner is so critical.

It is here that we point out the high degree of importance to choose a builder/contractor that has ministry experience and preferably a heart for serving the church. This mutual respect for the mission of the church or ministry is essential and makes a remarkable difference in the success of the project and relationships. There will be comments such as, "Construction is construction regardless of the type or use of structure." This project philosophy is indicative of a firm that is not partnering with the church or the ministry to bring about a successful project for the benefit of the church and its mission of ministry. To this contractor, this is simply *another construction job.*

In the *traditional* delivery method, the contractor provides a lump sum contract with allocation of construction costs to the subcontractors generally provided in a sworn statement at the time of payment requests or construction draws. Under this method, the general contractor retains the subcontractors, marks up their price and passes this on to the owner/ministry. The subcontractors who will be under contract to the GC in this method have not had input prior to their pricing drawings. Their understanding of the ministry purpose/needs/goals has not been considered whatsoever. Similarly the church/ministry has not had any input from the critical team of key subcontractors.

Under this method of delivery, the church is subjected to *partnering* with firms that they generally do not have familiarity or a relationship with; who are brought into the project and chosen by the low bid contractor that is now under contract with the church.

Construction Management

The CM contractor is retained as an agent of the owner and delivers the construction project at a fixed fee for managing the construction process and participating as a team member. It is important that the CM is as engaged early-on as possible so they are able to provide value in design and construction expertise, engineering services, as well as schedule and budget input.

Under this delivery method, all subcontract prices are shared with the owner. This may also be referred to as open book, where the owner knows where costs are being allocated along the way.

There is no hidden *buy out* of the subcontractors; instead each subcontract price is negotiated, and the owner always knows the price and the identity of the firm being chosen for the particular trade area. The advantage in CM is the owner/ministry is informed as to all project costs and specifically where the funds are being allocated. There is still a competitive nature to the project as all subcontracts are based upon competitive bids being overseen by the CM in partnership with the owner throughout the bidding process.

In the construction management method, the subcontractors report directly to the CM, who is the owner's agent. In essence, under this method there is a system of checks and balances built into the process. There are similarities however to the traditional delivery method. Under CM, the owner warrants that the drawings are free from error and assumes this responsibility. There are significant liabilities that the owner will assume under this method of construction delivery.

Design/Build

Design/Build is a method of project delivery in which one entity (design/builder, i.e. master builder) enters into a single contract with the Owner to provide architectural/engineering design and construction services. This system is designed for owner convenience, efficiency and cost effectiveness. This is a *relationship driven model* that has key partners from the church and the design/build firm working together to fulfill the mission of the church/ministry. The design/builder delivers a successful project by providing single source responsibility, fulfilling multiple parallel objectives, including planning, designing, budgeting and scheduling for a timely completion. With Design/Build, the owner is able to focus on scope and making timely decisions, rather than on coordination between architect, separate engineer, separate builder and multiple subcontracting firms. This method places the responsibility for quality and detail to the Design/Build team, allowing the ministry to focus on ministry responsibilities.

In more detail, Design/Build avoids the adversarial relationships inherent to the design-bid-build and sometimes the construction management delivery scenario. Design/Build is a parallel process whereby the required information, such as fulfilling ministry needs, site, specifications, budget, etc., are developed in parallel with all team members, including and most importantly the church as owner. The contract most often includes a lump sum project cost, based upon a specified scope of work. Price is only affected if the scope changes. The team includes civil, structural and mechanical engineers, as well as all other sub trades who have Design/Build experience and a long standing understanding of the relationship driven Design/Build method of construction delivery.

These subcontractors are often brought in on the project early to lend their expertise to the developing design. These professionals, by being involved in the process, will have an important understanding of the goals of the church as communicated to them by the Design/Build firm. In this method, the Design/Build firm has been working with the church from the beginning, from feasibility through complete design. They will have a thorough understanding of the preferences and DNA of the church that they are partnering with.

A church/ministry, by its very nature, is people-oriented and so is the experienced Design/Build firm. The understanding and respect developed in this type of partnership is the very glue to a successful project.

A key distinction with Design/Build is that the team begins to collaborate from day one, with the leaders and key members of the ministry, all working together on behalf of the ministry to build the best project possible. A question that might be posed is, "Why would anyone desiring to build a wellplanned project wait until almost the end of the process to determine the most important member of the team, the builder?"

" Why would anyone desiring to build a well planned project wait until almost the end of the process to determine the most important member of the team, the builder?"

When utilizing Design/Build and developing a working relationship with the design/builder, the owner has the advantage of knowing that both design and contract costs have been determined through cumulative and careful planning by an informed and engaged team. When compared to other disengaged delivery methods, which determine cost as the last step and with limited, if any, relationship, we see a striking difference.

The good news is that when professional companies work together in a design/build or CM arrangement and in the spirit of getting the job done with excellence, positive results will occur and adversarial relationships will be minimized or removed. It is acceptable to disagree as long as the questions can be addressed professionally and in a spirit of working together for a common goal. This demeanor is particularly important given the fact that we are embarking on building a God honoring tool for the work of expanding the Kingdom.

From a business and fiduciary perspective, when utilizing design/build, churches and ministry leaders are able to assure to their congregations that important checks and balances are built into the process. This is accommplished by the team working together in harmony for the benefit of the owner.

Summary:

Some will assert that without seeking multiple alternatives for pricing out the project that the church may not be getting the best possible price. Could this be a false assertion? As pointed out in design/build, the ministry is provided with a professional, cost effective and qualified team that is informed as a collaborative team of what the church, school or ministry is setting out to accomplish. Seeking a *lowest price* is often successful at the end of the bid process. Low price undoubtedly is attention getting. When a disengaged, uninformed group of companies works simply to develop a low price, the innocent owner often gets just that... a low price where the age old statement "you get what you pay for" or perhaps do not pay for overtakes the process.

When quality, thoroughness and long term relationship is overlooked, the process that could have been a successful God honoring collaborative and enjoyable process probably turns sour. Cutting corners and working quickly so as to move on to the next project often occurs. Churches should thoroughly trust their builder and design team and know that they are concerned for the current and long term success of the project. The end of the project is not the time to research and learn about your builder and whether or not their team can perform in a timely manner and be there for future questions and assistance.

Your ministry represents the sacrifices of many families. Your own research and due diligence in choosing an appropriate team to work with your church can have long term consequences.

The delivery method that the building team is most comfortable

27

with is the one that should be used. Design/Build is a seamless, cost effective method for ministries to plan, design and build their project. It is vital that you have open input into every phase of the design. It is also practical to know, trust and totally rely on your design and construction team to be entirely responsible for your project. Lastly, a single source of responsibility is better able to maintain schedule, safety and owner requirements.

When choosing the construction delivery method that is most appropriate for you, it is important to determine that the firm you choose to work with can assure that they are able to perform or has effective access to all of the following disciplines:

- *Timely and effective project accounting*
- *Availability of labor*
- *Code analysis experience*
- *Construction feasibility*
- *Contracts*
- *Document control*
- *Energy conservation*
- *Engineering*
- *Estimating*
- *Fast tracking*
- *LEED elements consideration*
- *Life cycle cost analysis*
- *Planning*
- *Preliminary and final estimate*
- *Project management*
- *Purchasing*
- *Risk mitigation*
- *Safety*
- *Scheduling*
- *Scope control*
- *Selection of subcontractors*
- *Sustainability*
- *Value engineering*

Next, we introduce the PBS 5-Step Delivery Process that lays the groundwork for the planning and development of a ministry project.

PROVERBS 8:33

Listen to my instruction and be wise,
do not disregard it.

"After having worked as a contractor and as a building inspector, and now as a church building team chairman, it was a pleasure to work with PBS, who is an honest building contractor that put in the extra effort to get the project done on time."

Dan Smits, Building Committee Chair
Thorn Creek Reformed Church

"We have been very pleased with everything that PBS has done on our renovation project. The work has been first rate and the workers have been easy to work with. I have been especially impressed with the patience and flexibility of the PBS team."

Pastor Matthew Baugh
First Congregational Church of Lockport

"The design and construction exceeded our expectations."

Father George Schopp
St. Peter Claver

"We appreciated our relationship with PBS from the planning of the project through construction. The PBS professionals worked closely with us to ensure we were getting the right building for the application we desired. PBS's seamless process of design/build allowed greater communication throughout, and in the end, gave us a quality product that will serve our mission to Grow Deep and Reach Wide for years to come."

Derick Miller
Senior Pastor - River Valley Christian Fellowship

PROVERBS 12:15

The way of fools seems right to them,
but the wise listen to advice.

CHAPTER 2
The PBS 5-Step Building Process

HOW TO BEGIN the Church Building Process? Countless groups have met for hours, days, weeks and months to discuss this question.

A very small percentage of churches build, add on or repurpose their facilities more than once or twice in a generation. Generally pastors and church leaders seek out people within their church family to begin a planning or building team. In most cases they also seek outside advice to assist in the important planning and feasibility phase.

Involving a design/build firm at this important stage early in the process can pay financial and space utilization dividends for years to come. Trust and an open relationship are a key at this point in the process. Developing a trust relationship with a design/build firm is much like allowing a Dad to catch his trusting toddler when the toddler jumps off a table into Dad's arms. The church has to allow and entrust the professionals to do what they do best. However that is not to say that the church just blindly allows the design/builder free reign, but it is to say that, working in partnership together, the Church trusts the expertise and experience of a good design/build team.

Trust That Leads to The Wedding

This trust is much like a marriage for a significant period of time. The courtship occurs during the time where the design/build team

31

asks questions and learns of the church's dreams and aspirations. The engagement occurs when the church has contracted with the design/builder to develop planning schemes and illustrations during which time the church and the design/builder deepen their trust and relationship with one another. Both the church and the design/builder, much like transferring trust when first coming to faith, must be open and totally honest with one another. This is not a time for wavering or second thoughts about one another. You have now both gone through many meetings and learned of the strengths that will significantly impact your ministry. This time together can be significant and eventually leads to the actual wedding. On the wedding day, the church and the design/builder enter into a design build contract triggering the final design phase leading to construction.

This courtship, engagement and wedding concept and the churches *transferring trust to the design/builder* is vital to the Faith Building concept.

Faith Building will ask and answer key questions as to how to build a ministry tool. It will assist your ministry to focus and head in a direction that will help you ask and then answer the important questions.

Following the **Faith Building** concept can save a Ministry literally hundreds of hours of combined volunteer efforts as you determine what initial steps to take and how to accomplish subsequent critical steps.

Here is an interesting thought: most churches have someone in the church or someone that knows someone that has built a building at one time or another. You will need to answer this tough question: does that someone or those construction and design contacts have experience and expertise in designing and building ministry facilities? It is vital to remember that you are not building a doctors' office, a warehouse or a retail center. A church is specifically in the people business. Knowing the important steps in developing a facility that engages, motivates and leads people to focus on eternity is extremely important.

Key concepts and questions for your leadership or building team:

- *Does your design/builder also have experience in ministry and leadership in their own individual churches?*

- *Does your design/build team serve and work for eternal purposes?*

- *Are they understanding of the importance beyond this just being another building project?*

This is essential. Designing and building a place of worship is a completely different process in terms of how the project is conceived, developed and finally constructed. The Ministry will have multiple groups of people working separately and together to compile information to answer literally hundreds of questions that will need to be addressed at some point in time. An important difference to note is that most designers and builders are not accustomed to working in this environment and, even more importantly, they may not understand the goals of the ministry, or have the skill sets necessary to work with a ministry comprised of multiple groups.

The answer to the question as to how to begin the process to design and build a church or faith building (school, multi-purpose building, etc.) will be addressed in the PBS 5-Step Process. These procedures are proven methods that will assist in understanding the design and construction process. There are important nuances in these processes and understanding these nuances is the key for projects to conclude on time and on budget and be able to meet your ministry goals successfully.

For example, it has been shown over-and-over again that many groups, such as banks, accountants and attorneys do not fully understand the construction process. This is not meant as a criticism but often when an attorney is approached about the construction delivery process, they allude to the fact that the only way to achieve the best price is through competitively bidding the project, as they assume that the construction management delivery method, and/or the design/build method, do not competitively bid the project or are not seeking *qualified* pricing. Of course, as has been discussed previously in this book, this is inaccurate. It is common that when a church's counsel or attorney has the opportunity to thoroughly review the design/ build method and corresponding contractual documents, the counsel endorses the method and approves the process as the most appropriate for ministry facilities. This example emphasizes the importance of seeking advice that is informed.

The PBS 5-Step Building Process

Step 1: Scope Development
Project Conception: Where ministry vision is defined.

The first step is developing a comprehensive Scope. What is the vision for the project? It is at this step where initial, vitally important questions are asked and answered. These answers will direct PBS to guide the ministry toward first steps in space development with an eye on master planning for the future. The questions that PBS will be asking will help summarize the magnitude and extent of the project. Many times when we ask these questions, the response is, "we had not considered that, or that is really important for the future."

For example,
- *What do you hope to accomplish from a ministry perspective by embarking upon this project?*

- *Is it a new ministry or outreach at a different location?*

- *Is it a renovation or expansion of the present facility?*

- *What is an affordable budget? From a budget perspective, will you be better positioned by phasing the project?*

- *Is it a major renovation?*

- *Do you have to purchase land?*

- *What about parking, local codes?*

- *Timeline: Will the project be ongoing during or after a capital stewardship campaign? When do you need or desire to take occupancy to the new or renovated facility?*

- *If moving to a new campus, what are the plans for the existing facility?*

- *What is the size of your congregation now and anticipated growth rate after project completion?*

- *What are your key demographic indicators? How will these factor into the design of your new building?*

- *What is your current and available debt service?*

To assist in verifying and confirming demographic makeup and trends, PBS will often provide a demographic study for you that includes the surrounding area within a certain radius of influence for your congregation. Also, a ministry survey analysis will be provided to take a snapshot of your entire ministry to assist in determining the best solution for your needs. Determining answers to these important questions will require communication. Let's consider the planning process: planning is an art, but it is also all about communicating; planning is a process where the vision is identified, and then the steps to accomplish the vision are addressed. The final shape and form, timeline, and other issues are not specifically determined; what is determined is the SCOPE of the project relative to the vision.

Initial planning leads to the second step where you will be assessing funding capacity. It is important to determine early on whether or not the ministry can afford to build what they have identified as their vision.

Step 2: Design / Development / Financial Feasibility
Creativity: Where budget and vision come together.

The answers in Step 1 will lead to this important second group of questions which deal with total project costs and affordability. This is where the scale of the vision must meet the budget for the project.

PBS will guide you through the process of how to plan financially to be in a position to complete your project. This is a critical step.

Most designers and builders tend to avoid or shy away from addressing financial requirements and solutions. More than one church has been told by designers or contractors to "call them back when you have adequate funds." That should not be an acceptable answer.

A logical process includes addressing all of the questions of the project, including funding. By first understanding and defining the scope of work based upon needs and wants, an accurate budget can be developed, and funding alternatives suggested. Solutions can then be identified, presented, discussed and then adopted to effectively launch and continue the planning process.

PROVERBS 13:10
Where there is strife, there is pride,
but wisdom is found in those who take advice.

For example, the average timeline of a project is eighteen to twenty four months from the time PBS first begins to work with its ministry customers to the time when your building is readied for occupancy. This is a practical timeline that allows for all of the steps to occur, from planning, to funding, to design and construction.

As we have already discussed, there are multiple directions that a church or school might take to facilitate building needs. An existing building can be repurposed, added on to or construction might be phased over multiple phases to achieve long term goals.

Occasionally for some churches, the best solution is not to build.

You might say, "This is a peculiar statement coming from a company who designs and builds ministry tools for a living." It is important to recognize that if any ministry is compromised at the cost of expanding facilities, then together, we should ask if the church would be better off postponing space expansions? Buildings can and should be effective tools for evangelism, but let's plan properly together and safeguard that we are not putting day to day ministries and outreach in jeopardy to launch a building campaign.

Once again phasing can be a sensible alternative. Depending on individual circumstances it may be practical and advantageous to consider a phased approach. Under this approach you may choose to complete the most important spaces that help achieve your immediate goals. Then, as funding and giving come in line with needs the church can move to the next phase.

Remember, combined with prayer and meaningful communication among your leadership team and design builder, effective steps can be identified to assist you in accomplishing the vision that you have developed.

Step 3: Construction Documents
Construction Timeline: Where plans are confirmed and approved and permitting is completed.

The construction document phase is where the vision is communicated by developing diagrams of the work, often referred to as the working drawings, or construction documents. Included in these construction documents are the detailed specifications for the project.

These documents are used to obtain building permits, purchase materials and schedule manpower, all of which will allow the project to move forward. Through the process thus far, this is often the most exciting part for the church and the entire design/build team. The light has turned GREEN to GO!

The input from the various committees, which will be discussed further on in this book, continues. Now the questions are different and more specific leading to decisions that will have a dramatic impact on the feeling of the space through color and texture, lighting, sound and signage. All of this is done within the scope of the vision and the budget.

Once all documents are signed and completed, the plan is put into action and permitting begins.

Step 4: Construction
Safety, Quality and Service: When the project is built.

Simply put, here is where *vision* becomes *reality*. The construction phase starts, which means activity begins on your job site. A continuous stream of subcontractors will enter the picture. PBS, as your design/builder, is orchestrating the entire process of converting the design and construction documents to brick, mortar, steel and concrete.

Construction is very calculated with simultaneous activities and disciplines occurring in tandem. Certain activities must be completed before others can start with some encountering schedule overlap.

The construction phase includes a laser focus on safety of the workmen and all of the visitors that are on site. For this reason PBS issues specific instruction and safety equipment to those that will be viewing the work for the ministry at appropriate times. The PBS team will include trained professionals and certified sub contractors and suppliers. Their training during the certification process will enable them to serve on the project in concert with each trade, the design builder and you, the owner, with your best interests at the center of the project construction process.

Step 5: Occupancy

Follow-up and Details: A celebration of the completed project.

Celebration is the operative word. It truly is a celebration when the first group of people meet for worship or study in a newly renovated, expanded or green field facility. It is a journey to get to this point, but it is worth it, for in the end there is a new tool for the advancement of the Kingdom.

Much needs to be accomplished to make "taking occupancy" of the project an exciting time for all involved. We will discuss this later in this book.

Summary:

The 5-Step Visioning Process that PBS utilizes is just that; a way to visualize the steps that must be taken to get from the very first question of thinking about a new ministry to actually meeting, worshiping and studying together in the completed space.

The ministry of construction is very much like prayer; it is partly an individual effort and partly a communal effort that expresses thoughts and emotions all directed at achieving a goal. The ministry of construction at PBS includes all the people that will be designing and building the building, as well as those who will be using the new facility.

There are many other details in the PBS 5-Step Visioning Process, and a key element is the building committee or team that deals with the needs and wants of the ministry. It is where everything begins.

Next, identifying the NEEDS and WANTS and how they relate to the budget.

"It was a pleasure for me to wholeheartedly recommend Professional Building Services (PBS) as a general contractor, and specifically, as in our case, general contractor for a church building project. The PBS team came up with many creative and attractive design solutions and also many cost saving solutions. We are very pleased with the quality of their work."

Christian C. Spoor, Pastor Emeritus
Living Springs Community Church

PROVERBS 14:29
Whoever is patient has great understanding,
but one who is quick tempered displays folly.

CHAPTER 3
Needs and Wants of Ministry Design

LET'S FORM A COMMITTEE OR TEAM. *Really, are you sure?*
Never have braver words been spoken. Being on a committee
or building team carries a significant responsibility for the
members that agree to be on the team. A building committee
has responsibilities that it shoulders, and the first, and a very
important responsibility deals with the building budget. The
second one deals with making sure that the church or school get
what they want, what they envision and what they have been
praying for.

It's important to understand that building teams need guidelines.
In our experience at PBS there are several important questions
that need to be addressed to ensure success. Remember this
is a group that is charged with fulfilling the wishes of all of the
members and key stakeholders of the ministry.

Questions include the following:
- *The size of the building committee?*
- *Who is on the committee?*
- *Who on the committee is handling what?*
- *Who from the committee will be the point of contact?*

An important function of the committee will be reporting regular
progress to the congregation. Your *building team members* must
have excellent communication skills... not necessarily exceptional
construction savvy... but are able and willing to carefully
communicate. The congregation as a whole certainly has an

41

important stake in the project, so updating and communicating events and milestones that are reached is key to building enthusiasm in the project.By keeping everyone up to date, staff will have the opportunity to recruit and position ministry teams and volunteers that the church intends to utilize. Together you will be in an informed position to be able to react and complete tasks for the important dates that you, as owner, will be planning and accomplishing as you take occupancy of the new space. This, as mentioned above, builds excitement and *ownership* for the important tasks ahead.

A challenge for building teams is to make sure that the individual members see important elements from a similar point of view – apples are apples, oranges are oranges regardless of the flavor. This insures that votes are being based upon the same criteria of understanding.

Some realities: Committees or building teams are dynamic and require managing... specifically managing expectations. Everyone

PBS CHURCH VISIONING GROUP

Project: River Valley Christian Fellowship
Reporting Period: February 4th – February 8th
Prepared By: Bryan Reiser of PBS Church Visioning Group

OVERALL PROJECT SUMMARY
We are working towards enclosure as exterior wall framing has begun.

WEEKLY UPDATE – FEBRUARY 4TH – FEBRUARY 8TH

Tasks Accomplished
- Gabled roof at entry has been constructed and insulated nailer applied
- Vented fascia has been installed
- Rectangular duct is being installed
- Transformer has been set
- Preparations for exterior wall framing are underway
- Exterior wall framing has begun
- Welded metal door frames have been delivered
- Exterior windows have been delivered

has a different set of experiences, and when one takes a position on something, the others may agree, but actually think it means something else. Decision making is also an important part of the committees' work. Successful decision making is often based on accurately defining the situation or question, and that is where experience comes to play. As described in Chapter Two, the PBS 5-Step Process goes to the heart of the big picture which provides a backdrop for proper decision making.

In designing and building a new facility it is important to establish guidelines. These guidelines wash the gray areas and provide clarity for all those involved.

A committee or building team, to be effective, must decide how to decide.

One heartfelt reason for participating in writing **Faith Building** the book, is that the PBS Church Visioning Group has been blessed to have had experience with this process through various types of projects. We do not boast about having an exceptional number of projects. We have, however, had the humble honor of partnering with a number of exceptional ministries. Seeing a project through successfully is tremendously satisfying. Following proven methods will see you through to a successful project. This guideline has been developed for the benefit of churches, Christian Schools and ministry teams to use in effective planning and execution of the building process.

A method most often used to communicate information about the needs and wants of a church is through the committee or team who is tasked with the goal of working with the designer. The committee is responsible to the congregation for the success of the entire building project. The initial step that the PBS Church Visioning Group takes is to provide guidance to a committee or building team in setting up effective practices. This guidance is based upon observing the interaction of many different building teams. This experience is the critical starting point in developing effective plans for your new or expanded facility.

The building team will be asked to complete a number of strategic tasks in a timely fashion during the course of the project. Having said this, an effective starting point is considering the make-up of the team, bringing as many different skill sets as possible. Also, a chairperson should be elected that will serve as a point person in keeping things moving forward, including the overseeing of meetings.

A Secret of Successful Church Building...before even one shovel full of dirt is turned over, is that the church body must be in agreement as to the type of ministry or outreach it desires to focus on and what type of facility will best accommodate that work. PBS can help guide a church in this discovery process, first by listening to the church, then asking clarifying questions and, finally, making suggestions to properly implement these objectives.

The key to a successful building project is communication.

To further a concept previously discussed, it is important to allow and empower PBS as your design builder to *provide input* to the church on the steps required to bring the project to fruition. Allowing the professionals to paint the picture to your congregation or school assists your building team from a third person perspective to accomplish your goals.

Carve out time for the design builder to detail the planning, design, approval and permitting processes. Openly discuss and gain an understanding of the letting of trade contracts, the flow of required paperwork, etc. The more you as the customer understand, the better *partner* you will be throughout the project.

Teaming includes:

- *Assisting with strategic goal setting*
- *Allowing PBS as your design/builder to apply its process from the first meeting*

The Earlier the Better

Many discussions take place when a church decides to build. It cannot be stressed enough that one of the more important and early steps that will pay back a huge dividend throughout the project is to meet and talk openly with your design/builder. The earlier the better, as they will be able to provide your committee or building team with a roadmap of questions that must be addressed. This meeting, when attended by key leaders, will get the entire project started in the right direction.

One of the major advantages of identifying objectives early in the project is that PBS will be able to determine if your expectations match your budget. Consider that a project is going to take a year or longer to design and build. If it's discovered that funding will be short of the intended project budget, it may mean that phasing will need to be implemented. Potentially, if funding is not yet at a comfortable starting point, but within reach...then completing design and implementing fund raising events featuring the completed design will often energize the congregation to bring the funding to an appropriate starting point. Whatever happens, the important thing is that there is an informed perspective being exercised in the decision making process.

The building team is designed to provide a conduit of information from the church leadership to the designer. One of the things a designer is going to do is develop a Program that will utilize all the ideas leadership wants to be addressed in the new facility. This

45

is where *needs and wants* are outlined. As the project begins to take shape the questions are going to be more specific and more detailed, such as does this tile meet our needs, or do you like this tile better and why? What is our color scheme, etc.?

Summary:

The committee stays together during the entire process from design through construction. As the project moves through different phases they will be asked for more input and direction as they represent the nucleus of their church.

The next chapter, *Planning With Prayer*, covers the actual planning process that is used to gather the critical information needed to design your new ministry facility.

PROVERBS 15:22

Plans fail for lack of counsel,
but with many advisers they succeed.

"We have enjoyed our relationship with PBS; they have become our friends. We are pleased with our new building and now have an excellent tool to better serve CCC and the surrounding community."

Matt Summers, Pastor
Crossroads Christian Church

PROVERBS 16:3

Commit to the lord whatever you do,
and he will establish your plans.

CHAPTER 4
Planning With Prayer

"PLANNING WITH PRAYER" means just that. Prayer is an integral part of each and every step of PBS's planning process. God is the ultimate Master Architect and Builder, and being such, He is a God of details. Observing the world around us continually confirms this. The planning process involves a myriad of details from numerous sources that must be brought together to conceptualize, design and then build the final product (i.e. a new worship facility, an expansion or a renovation to an existing building).

PBS's first step in the *Planning With Prayer* process is to meet with the church leadership and begin building a working relationship with them. The PBS planning team will first *listen* to the ministry leadership's vision. What we learn from our time with your leadership team, in turn, will help to shape the direction of the new and/or expanded facility.

Things such as the specific ministry and size of required spaces, the projected size of the ministry and growth rate and the demographics of the congregation will be discussed. Multi-purpose spaces, cafés, open areas for fellowship and education will also be examined. It is during these initial meetings that the ministry leadership will come to understand that PBS will put the church's needs and desires ahead of PBS's bottom line and that, in overseeing their project, PBS will seek to honor God in its actions, as much as the church desires to do so. Seeking God's will together in prayer is vital at this early stage, not only for the church, but for PBS as well. Asking for God's wisdom and discernment, especially

49

in areas of uncertainty, is a course of action that will often bring wisdom that removes uncertainty. Once PBS has a thorough understanding of what the church desires, the process becomes somewhat complex. There are a multitude of items to consider, many of which are interrelated. Based on information obtained from the ministry, the PBS design team will begin to lay out a design for the facility, or perhaps more than one. However, there is more to this design phase than just creating a three-dimensional drawing to show the appearance of the finished facility.

The planning and design team must also consider:

- *The structural integrity of the design*
- *The site requirements and restrictions*
- *The municipal building codes*
- *The various permits to be obtained*
- *The effect that the new facility or expansion will have on the surrounding neighborhood*
- *In the case of an expansion, how the new design fits with the existing building*

Once a workable design has been developed, one that agrees with the ministry vision and all the physical requirements and restrictions of construction, PBS will provide complete design and construction costs prior to completing construction drawings to ensure what has been designed is consistent with the ministry budget.

During this entire stage of planning, prayer continues to be an integral and vital tool. It helps both the planning team and the ministry leadership to remain focused on the task at hand and the responsibility that comes with it.

At this point in the planning process, the PBS planning team will stress to leadership the necessity of being sure that the design which has been developed actually fulfills their vision.

This is not to say that changes cannot be made, but the further along in the construction process, the more costly major changes can be. Once again, prayer is vital to assure that the design chosen is within God's will.

Once construction drawings are released, the *Planning with Prayer* process moves to the letting of subcontracts. PBS awards contracts only to reputable contractors familiar with our process. We strive to maintain a good working relationship with each one of them. They then become an integral team working together to serve the PBS customer. PBS does not specifically evangelize to the contractors who work for them, but, in keeping with its desire to serve God, PBS openly identifies itself as a Christian-based company and, accordingly, deals with its subcontractors with integrity, honesty and fair play. This goes a very long way in assuring that the ministry's new facility has been built with the highest possible standards.

PBS's *Planning with Prayer* process runs throughout the life of the project from the moment of first contact to the *grand opening* of the completed facility.

PROVERBS 21:5
The plans of the diligent lead to profit
as surely as haste leads to poverty.

To churches planning or preparing to start a Building Project, the following suggestions are made:

A. *For those firms that you are considering, do not be timid in asking questions of them. It is unlikely that all members of your Church Building Committee will have an intimate knowledge of the construction business. Heed the manner*

51

and attitude in which the prospective builder answers your questions. Whom does he seem to be more genuinely concerned about? You and your church or their company? Always seek God's wisdom when meeting with a potential builder... wisdom to ask the right questions, wisdom to understand the answers and wisdom to discern the priorities of the potential builder. Then have faith that God will lead you to the right builder for your project. As we discussed early on in this book, the planning, design and construction period mirrors a marriage in many ways. It is vital that you choose the right partner.

B. *Once a builder has been selected to design and/or oversee your project, ask for a tour of some of the facilities that he has brought to fruition. This will give you a firsthand look at the workmanship he requires from the subcontractors working for him.*

C. *Understand exactly what services your builder of choice offers, his procedures in delivering those services and what responsibilities the church will have, if any, in helping to facilitate those services. If the Church Building Committee and the Builder's Team work together to build a relationship of mutual trust and respect and strive to maintain a common focus on issues at hand throughout the project, then successful completion of the project is guaranteed.*

D. *Invite God to every meeting and always listen to what He has to say.*

Summary:

Planning is the heart of the future project. Prayer is an integral part of each and every step of PBS's planning process.

Next, the financial part of developing a new ministry project is discussed with guidelines and important considerations.

PROVERBS 16:9

In their hearts humans plan their course,
but the lord establishes their steps.

"I was reflecting recently on God's providence with our building. I have seen prices dramatically increase recently. This brings me to thank God for his timing. Your commitment contributed to God allowing us to afford the building that we now enjoy. Thanks, Dale, for PBS' commitment and contribution. The outcome and end product was providential and being used well for the kingdom."

Bruce Koenigsburg
Parkview Community Church

PROVERBS 18:9
One who is slack in his work
is brother to one who destroys.

CHAPTER 5
Financial

PART OF THE FLOW OF A CONSTRUCTION PROJECT is the flow of money to the subcontractors and suppliers that are or will be providing goods and services. Along with this comes the protection of the ministry to ensure that they are receiving what they are paying for along with built-in safe guards for the protection of the sacrificial giving of the congregation.

Financing requires the ability to step back and look at the big picture. First, financing for a ministry project is critical in determining the successful completion of the project. For one, you are unable to begin the process until

It is imperative that we are prudent, wise and discerning while we consider the potential costs of ministry financing.

funding is available and can be released for the project. Proper and efficient management of funds is important, particularly when often a large part of the project is funded through consistent sacrificial giving. It is important to remember, we are instructed in the Word to be good stewards of what we have been entrusted with.

Luke 14:28 NIV: Suppose one of you wants to build a tower. Will he not first sit down and estimate the cost to see if he has enough money to complete it?

At PBS we believe it is important to safeguard our partner's investments with financial controls to ensure that all funding is allocated properly per the plans and specifications. PBS's financial manager has the responsibility of setting up accounts for each individual project which will include the preparation of a project sworn statement (commonly referred to as a contractor's statement), waivers of lien and all other appropriate documentation for the proper sequencing and disbursement of project funding.

While we bear a tremendous responsibility in the management of the ministry's sacrifices, we are also very careful to ensure that our project team remains in a strong financial position in order to serve each ministry in the manner it deserves. This is often not considered. You should want your design/builder to be in a good financial position on your project so that their focus stays on the thorough delivery of construction and not the *loss or slow flow of funding* through construction. Luke 10:7 For the worker deserves his wages.

It is important to be able to show at any point how and where the project funding is being distributed for the benefit of the leadership who are consistently communicating project progress updates to the congregation. Thorough and efficient management of each ministry's resources is of vital importance as we move into and through a project. PBS assumes responsibility when partnering with ministries for the sacrifice each of their ministry partners families have made. Regardless of the level of contribution each gift is a sacrifice.

Unity

Before you begin your search for project financing the following two questions must be asked and agreed upon by your ministry leadership:

A. *Is your leadership unified in their decision to move forward?*

It is important to consider scripture here of "where there is no vision the people perish."

   B. *Is your church family committed to moving forward with the leadership's vision and planning?*

While we want to walk in faith, it is imperative that the leadership has a good understanding of the congregation's ability to fund the necessary financing without compromising ministry.

PBS maintains strong relationships with the title companies that disseminate and approve payments as this assists us in maintaining an unencumbered/clean title for the church. There are also other critical project accounting methods such as our ability to have a full accounting of all partial and final waivers of lien including material waivers from suppliers. Of similar importance is our project payment schedule which will display exactly where funds are being allocated allowing the ministry to maintain strict accountability to the overall project financing.

Plan accordingly to ensure that any debt service will not hinder your ability to provide ministry and spread the Word.

Debt Service

In Proverbs 22:7 King Solomon shares with us that as the rich rule over the poor, so the borrower is servant to the lender. With this wisdom we are reminded to be careful of the potential bondage created by debt.

From a financing perspective, be as aggressive as you can, in alignment with your ministry's ability to service a note, in paying off the debt. The Lord spoke of money 2,350 times in the Bible, even more than *love*. He knew the impact that *money* would have on each of our lives including the blessings that it could create, as well as the deep pain it may cause based upon the decisions that we make. Scripture states that it is the *love* of money that creates evil. Use this time with your congregation to teach about God's plan for money in our lives and how we can all use it wisely to benefit the Kingdom.

Financing Solutions

Beyond your own congregation's commitments, you will want to consider funding sources that are of like mind, *equally yoked*, whereby they will have your ministry's best interests at heart. More often your best relationships will come from inner denominational funding or specific church funding sources that operate outside of the world of financial institutions, i.e. banks. Though still prudent and wise in the decisions they make, these resources are generally not answering to a "worldly" minded board and are more willing to rationalize your investment on a Kingdom level.

While purchasing a home one will more than likely incur debt; though, it is our responsibility as stewards of what the Lord has entrusted us with to purchase within our means. Having such a mindset within the ministry will allow for you to effectively service the debt while also continuing to expand HIS Kingdom.

Have them explain to your ministry leadership why they would want to fund your ministry. Hear their hearts. Inevitably, if the approving bodies (board of directors) have a like-mind you will receive valuable wisdom as well as a well-developed plan for your ministry project financing if they are a good fit for your ministry.

Another key element in project funding is the project schedule. For each project

PBS will develop a detailed project design and construction schedule which will highlight sequencing of all trades through project completion.

This is an effective tool which allows all of us to maintain a close eye on progress and its continued effect on project accounting. Site engineering and preparation will generally start the project off. When we get into *vertical* construction, we will be ordering and storing raw materials so that we have them ready to utilize. These material deliveries will be accounted for in the project schedule and consistent with our project accounting. Construction funds will generally be held in escrow (or some form of an earnings account) until there is a draw on the account. If possible, the desire is to have the available funds working as long as possible until they are necessary for construction.

As it relates to project scheduling and sequencing, PBS will maintain very close communications with the owner's representative through the project. It is important that those involved with the project from the church, maintain an eye on the construction schedule and how it progresses week to week, in order to be aware in advance of decisions that need to be made. Such decisions involve project related selections, communication to the congregation and ministry programming schedule(s) based on construction schedule changes and adjustments.

Ministries will see specific reports that keep them up to date and are necessary for project payouts. Any credible construction firm has a rather sophisticated job as it relates to the cost accounting process that brings this all together for the proper sequencing of project funding. This information should be shared up front with the ministry as well as what the lending institution and title companies will require.

Summary:

Unless a church or school is prepared to tackle the hard world of construction and deal with lightning fast decision making requirements, they should carefully consider what delivery method they are interested in. In the end it is important to decide what will be the most thorough, efficient and professional delivery system for the ministry. The traditional way of building has inherent conflict, as well as undisclosed prices. Inevitably, under this delivery method of architect, bid, build, you will rarely know where the dollars are being allocated. Overriding this however is the onerous responsibility for design documents and trusting that all parties, although totally independent of one another, will work together for your benefit.

If your ministry is seeking a different method of delivery that is based upon practical principals of delivery, then the PBS 5-Step Visioning Plan is an alternative that will help you gain insight into the process that you may never know about until it is too late under alternate delivery methods. PBS will bring together those who are of like mind and who have a heart for the ministry of construction.

This is evidenced by way of their mission statement which reads:

"PBS is a design/build firm dedicated to
providing solutions that focus on integrity and consistency
and building authentic relationships in order to
exceed our customer's expectations."

"Not only were we novices, we were skeptical. However the approach of PBS, who became the design/build team we contracted with, immediately alleviated our apprehensions. They listened to our building team as each expressed the dreams and vision of this future church building."

Greg Eilders, Pastor
Peoples Church

PROVERBS 21:5
*The plans of the diligent lead to profit
as surely as haste leads to poverty.*

CHAPTER 6
Closeout

THE TERM CLOSEOUT relates to the end of the project, and is the final step as the various contractors and subcontractors complete their work and exit stage left, as they say in the theater. You are nearing the culmination of the project, where you will begin using the facility, coming together to worship, teach and learn.

Misunderstandings can occur about the meaning of *closeout*. As the contractor nears the end of the project, he will prepare a punch list, which shows what remaining work the different subcontractors and vendors must do to complete their contract. Completion of work triggers being paid in full for their work. Closeout is also closely tied to *substantial completion*, which is defined as:

Closeout requires PBS to coordinate many ongoing activities simultaneously.

"The stage in the progress of the work where the work or designated portion is sufficiently complete in accordance with the contract documents so that the owner can occupy or utilize the work for its intended use."

The date of substantial completion is an important date for the owner and for the design/builder as it defines endings and beginnings. It is a handoff date that says that the owner is now taking responsibility for the operation of the entire building, such as HVAC, parking lot, the building security and maintenance. The date also impacts certain warranties as to when they start.

63

And the date can impact when final funds are paid out to the subcontractor team.

Once arriving at substantial completion the owner/ministry can occupy and start using the space. Often, use of the space is granted based on the fact that any punch list items will be completed in an agreed amount of time. At this point, any unfinished work will not impact the safe usage of the new facility.

PBS has a system in place to insure that punch lists are completed on time by all subcontractors. The proper procedure for closeout is actually very simple and mandates suppliers and subcontractors to comply without any question. The punch list is ongoing from day one on the job site. As each and every subcontractor completes their portion of the work, the project manager walks the project and prepares a punch list with the subcontractor at that time, not waiting for the end of the project. This is particularly critical when the finish work is being completed as that is where the greatest potential for punch list or completion items will occur. By faithfully monitoring the punch list in an ongoing basis, the closeout goes smoothly so that the builder doesn't have to spend an extensive amount of time having the original subcontracting team return to the site to complete some portion of the work.

There are several activities that occur during closeout:

- *General description of the closeout requirements*
- *Final acceptance requirements*
- *Project cleaning*
- *Substantial completion acceptance*
- *Occupancy by owner*
- *Final payment*
- *Completion of the work per technical specifications*
- *Phase acceptance*

- *As-Built record drawings if appropriate*
- *Operating and maintenance manuals*
- *Final release of claims and liens*
- *Delivery of warranty package*

Summary:

If you want to determine the strengths of a design/builder, check his references as to project closeout. That will tell the story. How the project ends truly defines the *character* of the builder.

In the next and final chapter, an important *Faith Building* concept is discussed - the *Ministry of Construction*.

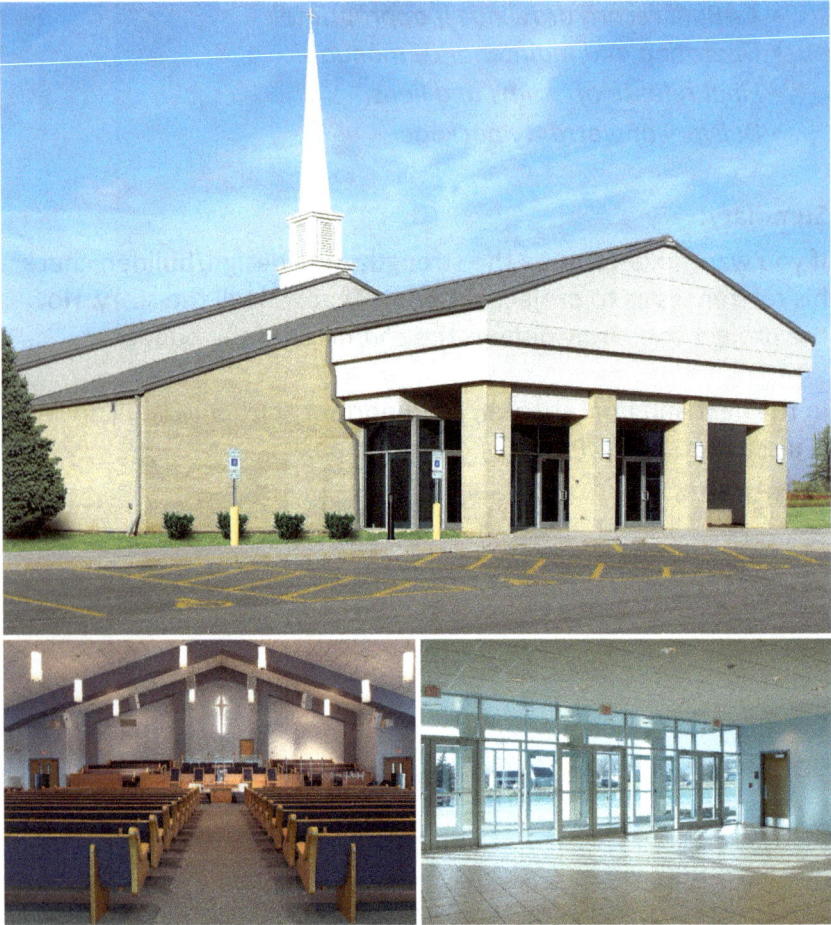

At the dedication ceremony, Reverend Martin exclaimed that "the project was made possible by the endless efforts of our friends at Professional Building Services. Our standing in this facility is testimony to their hard work. This has been a job well done and to the Glory of God. We give heart felt thanks, to our friends and co-workers in Christ at PBS."

Reverend Martin
St. Paul Missionary Baptist Church

PROVERBS 24:7
Put your outdoor work in order and get your fields ready;
after that, build your house.

CHAPTER 7
Ministry of Construction

YOU ARE PROBABLY CURIOUS as to what does "Ministry of Construction" mean? A good way to understand the answer is to first look at the pure definitions of the words ministry and construction.

min·is·try
n.pl. min·is·tries

1. a) The act of serving.
   b) One that serves.

2. a) The profession, duties, and services of a minister.
   b) The period of service of a minister.

con·struc·tion
n

1. a) The act or process of constructing.
   b) The art, trade or work of building

2. a) A structure, such as a building, framework, or model.
   b) Something fashioned or devised systematically

Based upon these two definitions, we can develop the definition that *Ministry of Construction* is the art of constructing a place where ministry can occur. Why this is important?

Typical construction is very much a profit driven timeline of activities based upon low bidders, all of whom want to get on and off the job as quickly as possible so they can move on to the next project. This is the opposite of what ministry is all about. For the most part, with this worldly mind set there is little, if any, intent of developing relationships and working together. Sure, folks are put into a position where they have to work together, but generally only as directed by the contract documents.

The above might be an extreme example, but the point is, this is not the way to build a faith building. It is the opposite; the *Ministry of Construction* is all about creating an environment that is, in itself, conducive to the Christian spirit of working together, helping others and working toward a common goal of peace and understanding. As you may have guessed, this, unfortunately, is not construction in the normal sense of the word.

Ironically enough we once had a pastor who mentioned that this building (his worship facility) is just a business. We found this quite interesting and honestly quite disturbing as we feel that what we are doing together is Kingdom Work and not just another day at the office.

PBS has been blessed to develop a Ministry of Construction that was developed to address the needs and goals of the ministry. We take these needs and goals and put them in a definable scope, develop a budget and timetable and then work with the members of the church to develop input and an understanding of the various spaces. We determine how they are used and how they may function in multiple ways.

PBS Ministry of Construction Mission Statement

The *Ministry of Construction* provides a means of sharing our faith in Jesus Christ with the construction workers on the jobsite. We will minister through friendliness, kindness, relationship building and gratitude using a wide variety of actions, which prayerfully may open a door to sharing our spiritual life.

While it is common to want to dive directly into what it *might* cost, as this is our nature, we want to educate the ministry that if you ask all the appropriate questions, build trust with a design/build firm, such as PBS, through this experience you will know and feel that you are being treated fairly. In the end, you will inevitably have a tremendous resource for the journey you are about to embark upon. There will always be someone that is willing to be, or appear to be, *less costly*. Those are often the projects that have large cost overruns disguised as unpleasant surprises and change order demands as a project nears completion. Select wisely for the benefit of your congregation. Do not settle for price without value! Build trust and relationship with someone that has built those same relationships with others and is intent on building a tool for the expansion of the Kingdom.

There are cautions in which we would be remiss in not pointing out. Consider the following: churches can be targets for greed, carried out by unscrupulous construction providers. Firms will assemble a bid noting the "fuzzy...or not so clear" areas in design drawings where one could debate about what the construction documents mean. They put a price together based upon the cost of the project, or below cost, and, unfortunately, after being awarded the contract, may begin to present the designer with change orders – one after the other. This is a remarkably common occurrence, and is obviously a recipe for adversarial relationships.

Thankfully, that is not how we at PBS do business, and that is not how you should expect to do business during your construction project.

Talk with those *others*. Do your due diligence. How was it working with XYZ in the preliminary planning, vision casting and through the entire construction process? Remember nothing will ever be perfect other than the Love of Christ. Work with someone who is humble enough to admit a mistake, but also wise enough to determine a solution. In this you will find the most qualified candidate to partner with your ministry.

Make sure that whomever you are working with is of like mind with your leadership team. Be careful of firms who indicate and may have *built a few churches*. We are not just building buildings; we are building tools for the Kingdom. It is imperative that the firm that you are going to inevitably spend many months with be of like-mind in accomplishing building a tool for effective ministry.

An Analogy

A family was adding on to their home, and it was a very substantial construction project that would mean the contractor would be there every day for six months from early in the morning until five or six o'clock at night. The family asked the designer: How do we select the right contractor when the prices are all about the same?

The designer's answer was, select the contractor whom you would want to move in and live with you for the six months duration of the construction project. The point the designer was making was that there is more to consider aside from price. There is value in the relationship, of ethics, of honesty of wanting to do what is right. When the family reflected on this, they knew exactly which contractor to hire.

The same can be said when selecting your design/builder for your ministry – price is certainly important, but there is much more to consider than price. There is the value, or shared values, of the relationship. Will your design/builder have the integrity to serve you years after completion of the project? What is the value of knowing that they will be there for you whatever the need may be long into the future. Are they providing you with a thorough all inclusive service?

Think about these questions when interviewing a design/builder:

- *Are they involved with their own home church ministries?*
- *Have them explain how they worship and their ministry style.*
- *Do they intimately understand worship style and settings?*
- *Do they understand worship ministry?*
- *Do they understand the intricacies of children/youth ministries, layout, safety, etc.?*

Ask any of these questions, and you will undoubtedly learn if and/or at what level they understand ministry, and if they share the same values as you. When they answer, do they hesitate and have to think of what they are going to say, or is their answer part of who they are and what they enjoy participating in. You are the customer! You deserve to serve your church or school by choosing a design/builder who intimately understands what your ministry is all about. They should be professionals in the design and construction of the tools to house and facilitate *what you do in ministry.*

When this plan comes together properly, construction will start and everyone is blessed with the feeling that it really is a team effort. A sincere and engaged design/builder will want the same dreams and desires as you do. At PBS for example, key employees are also ministry leaders.

Exercising the key elements in *The Ministry of Construction* is a proven method to meet the needs of the people and their dreams with the same Christian spirit that they have.

Yes, this concept of *Ministry of Construction* is different, but PBS is not afraid to be different. Yes, we are professional designers and builders, but ministry is part of what we are called to and committed to do every day.

71

Key Areas of Participation By the Church

This ministry may be the only gospel display that some of the workers on a project or delivery men, etc. will ever experience. We have seen where our church customers have attracted workers to become interested in their churches and eventually come to faith, membership and service in their churches. What a wonderful opportunity to reach out and serve!

How might the church do this?

Here are just a few possibilities:

- **Prayer Warriors**: *Pray at the job site as consistently as you would like. Pray specifically for the construction crews and continuously for the church body as the renovation, expansion or new construction takes shape.*

- **Encouragement**: *Thank, praise and encourage workers on the site. Have Sunday schools, small groups, office, and administration send notes of thanks and encouragement to the team of workers.*

- **Holy Graffiti**: *Write uplifting messages on the steel or concrete that will eventually be covered up with messages of thanks or encouragement.*

- **Lunches**: *Host lunches for the workers to exemplify hospitality to them from your ministry.*

- **Hot Coffee**: *Provide coffee to the workers, whereby any church staff or church members can take part and build relationships with the workers, showing the Love of Christ.*

- **Invite them to Worship**: *Extend invitations to worship to the workers.*

- **Construction Tours**: *Host tours of the site during construction so that members can appreciate the work of the builders.*

- **Worker Appreciation:** *Host an appreciation event for the workers.*

- **Resolve Disagreements**: *Resolve disputes and/or misunderstandings biblically.*

- **Fulfill your Commitments**: *Demonstrate to the workers that Ministry is in construction as well. While from their perspective they might "just be doing their job" they are involved with the construction of a tool that has eternal significance.*

- **Car Wash**: *Ask secondary students to periodically wash workers' cars.*

- **Day of Gratitude**: *Plan a special Day of Gratitude and invite the workers to thank them.*

What an exciting opportunity to serve our Lord through serving the workers He is sending to our site.

Summary:

The traditional way of building can unfortunately be steeped in conflict as well as undisclosed prices. Unless a ministry is ready to tackle the hard world of construction and go blow for blow as the different trades come through, a partnership with a design/build firm that has a heart for ministry is vital.

If your ministry wants a different way to proceed that is based upon the Christian spirit, then the PBS 5-Step Visioning Plan will help you gain an insight into the process that you may never know about until it's too late. PBS brings together those who have the similar values and dreams that you do.

"When people are so attracted to a place that they want to just come and see it, that's architectural evangelism."

Pastor Darren Sloniger
Founding Pastor West Ridge Community Church

PROVERBS 16:3

*Commit to the lord whatever you do,
and he will establish your plans.*

CONCLUSION

THE KEY QUESTION to consider in building a ministry facility is; who is it that you are partnering with to see that the vision is understood, interpreted correctly in the construction documents and then delivered in the construction process? Consider these characteristics as you search for a design/build firm:

1. *Trust*
2. *Consistency*
3. *They are "all in" (their desire is to serve the ministry)*
4. *Thorough*
5. *They appear to listen more than they "tell"*
6. *They are visually more relational than transactional in their service to you. Their desire to serve is completely evident in how they communicate and in the manner that they deliver.*

PBS is sensitive to ministry and vision casting. They serve by providing significant resources to meet these goals of your overall ministry VISION.

As an encouragement, their recommendation would be to see the construction progress in person. As important as it is to pay attention to the weekly updates that are put together by PBS, it is equally important to physically see the progress first hand on a regular basis. This can dramatically help with schedule and project close out as any changes that a committee may want to make during the course of construction can be made at the correct time, rather than at the end when it can be challenging to make the change, cost prohibitive or detrimental to the project schedule.

Drawing on the experience gained by being involved with planning, designing and building ministry facilities over the years can be a great resource in dealing with the intricacies of changing dynamics within ministry leadership. This can include the personnel make-up of the board, rapid ministry growth and changing demographics.

Also, as an additional tool are the association resources and experience from an experienced group of affiliated church design/build firms and association certified church consultants through the National Association of Church Design Builders (NACDB). PBS is a leader in the NACDB and in consistent communication on behalf of its ministry partners.

PBS's value to a ministry customer is its desire to do what is best for the ministry and yes there will be times when this may come as a sacrifice. As a result, the ministry is being served with true and sincere commitment. This philosophy builds authentic relationships benefitting owners for years to come.

PBS recognizes that they are in a position of responsibility. They have strategically created an environment in their construction projects that employs a ministry of construction mentality. There is accountability. Our hope is that in this there is evidence of our striving to be servants to our customers and pleasing in the eyes of our Lord.

APPENDIX
Frequently Asked Questions
(or questions you should be asking)

All architects and construction managers are often asked a lot of questions regarding the process. But interestingly enough, sometimes, people interested in accessing the skill sets of various builders and designers don't really know the right questions to ask.

Here is a list of common questions asked of PBS. Observe the answers and use this as a source for evaluation.

1. **What is your background in ministry design?**

   PBS has been involved in ministry design from the beginning of our company. The very first project was an inner city Chicago church in the early 1990's. Since then we have been involved in the design and construction of well over 100 church or Christian School projects.

2. **We want to build. Can you help us raise the remaining funds that we need?**

   Yes. We can help you in building and launching programs that will raise funds both from inside the church and also externally throughout the community. We can introduce you to professionals with integrity in this field. We can coordinate and be a conduit of information as you save toward your goal. Importantly, we can provide budget estimates so you know how to formulate realistic goals, and we can suggest, if applicable, a phased approach, lowering the initial costs.

3. **Briefly describe the services your firm will perform verses those that will be performed by consultants?**

   PBS provides feasibility strategies and develops preliminary and conceptual drawings up through the final architectural design process. During final design we utilize the services of specialty design, such as HVAC, Plumbing, Structural, and Civil who have worked with PBS on ministry centered projects for many years. PBS then coordinates the entire design process, managing, and supervising suppliers and subcontractors and the flow of work during construction.

4. **Describe the processes the firm utilizes to investigate bidders to ensure they are qualified and equipped to satisfactorily complete a project?**
Most service providers are known to us from previous construction projects. We have a formal certification process specifically designed for those partnering with us on Church projects that will be administered by the NACDB.

Additionally, PBS qualifies their subcontractor list through a comprehensive Contractor Approval process that provides customer and banking references. All of our contractors are required to have an approved safety program and be properly insured and licensed.

5. **Describe how your firm handles contractors who perform work unsatisfactorily or fall behind scheduled deadlines, or who do not follow the plans and specifications?**
As soon as a concern surfaces, be it related to the schedule or a departure from the plans and specs, we thoroughly and aggressively pursue resolution. Often the problems are quite explainable, and after our due diligence, we are able to determine solutions. Proper project management will generally avert issues that require remedial action. It is our goal to assist all of our team to be successful.

6. **What is your philosophy regarding punch lists?**
The punch list does not start when the project is ended; the punch list starts as the project progresses and in earnest when the subcontractor is nearing completion of their portion of work. Our on-site project manager is constantly reviewing

the work as it proceeds noting anything that is a discrepancy from the plans and specs and correcting it then. We do not wait until the end of the project, for we want the final completion list to be minimal and flow fast and to allow for occupancy to occur on time. Monitoring the work as it is completed is very important.

7. **How do you incorporate technology needs into the ministry design?**

   To PBS, this is one of the most exciting areas of the design. PBS will partner with one of our NACDB expert firms in sound, lighting and acoustical design to interface with our electrical design team to achieve the goals that our customers wish to attain.

8. **What separates you from the other prominent ministry architects or design/build firms that have an emphasis in church building?**

   Understanding functionality and our team and company's belief that our calling is helping others achieve their ministry goals through architectural design and evangelism. PBS listens, partners and then provides. We will not dictate or tell you what you need. We will plan with you and for you to achieve the best design for your particular circumstance.

9. **What about Fees?**

   In design build, your contract price is firm and will only change should you desire for changes to be made. Our pricing and design fees are very reasonable. PBS is not an architectural firm. Design is only a step in the service of eventually constructing your building. Design fees therefore are significantly lower than what a typical architectural firm might charge. Our design schemes are generally inclusive of systems building construction methods that incorporate economical, aesthetically pleasing buildings. If you are desiring a cathedral, we will probably not be the best choice as your design/builder.

If you are preferring a creative, cost effective design, our experience will convert to fees that are attractive and affordable. With a design/build delivery method, we can control construction costs because of the continuity of single source responsibility.

10. **We hear the word "green" used a lot. Does that apply to us?**

    Yes. We have LEED certified personal on staff and the decisions we make are conscious of the environment. We can show you all the steps we take to make sure the construction methods and materials are sustainable.

11. **Why should I hire you?**

    PBS is a dedicated ministry design/builder. It is what we like to do; it is what we talk about doing at every office management meeting we have. We are interested in being the best of the best. We do not treat it as another market niche — but THE market niche for our company. We are passionate about serving our customers to their complete satisfaction. We believe that the building within which ministry is occurring is of eternal value. That matters to us greatly. Lastly, we are a successful provider of many completed ministry related buildings.

12. **We have a member who is experienced in construction and would like to volunteer his time. Can you incorporate him into the project and pass the savings to us?**

    Yes. Absolutely! The first thing is to get those interested in the process so we know when and where we can use their services. It will, however, be imperative that these proprietors or firms will be qualified by PBS then certified as a subcontractor to PBS. It will be necessary that they be licensed and insured.

13. **How long does it take to complete design and receive a permit? Is there a way to speed up the process of getting to the field?**

    The schedule is one of the first areas we are going to address. Under the right circumstances design/build allows us to "fast track" the project. If consensus on floor plan, elevations and key materials has been reached, it is possible that we can proceed with heavy construction (site development, excavation and foundation placement) possibly before subsequent construction documents are completed. For example, once calculations and engineering are complete, we can design the foundation, which means site work engineering, grading and foundation work can begin early.

14. **Will you use local contractors?**

    Yes. We prefer to use local contractors. It is important though that they are familiar with PBS' specialized method of construction delivery. We have been blessed with new suppliers added to our team because of their often being introduced to us by our church customers.

15. **Our building will be used in many different ways. It needs to be durable. What are some things you will incorporate into the design that will help the building look newer, longer?**

    Actually, this question gets into two different areas. One is the development of multi-use spaces, and the other is the functionality of the design over time. These are important construction cost and maintenance issues that will need to be dealt with realistically with church staff and programming personnel.

16. **We hear that LEED certified buildings can have higher upfront costs and may not be for us. However, we want to be conscious of our resources. What are some "green"**

design elements that we can use that may not be as costly as a full LEED certification?

You are absolutely right.

One of the hidden parameters of LEED is that a LEED building can add up to as much as 2% to 6% of the total buildings cost, and this is mostly due to the commissioning and documentation process required during permitting and the construction process.

17. **Can LEED practices be employed or can LEED oriented materials be incorporated into your project to achieve the benefit without the cost of certification?**

Of course.

A suggestion is a LEED checklist that allows us together to determine what is important to you, effective in terms of long-term sustainability and costs.

You may see articles in the building periodicals suggesting that "the building is an uncertified Silver building." What that is saying is, the building was designed and built to a standard that would have qualified for LEED silver, however, the owner chose to incorporate the attributes without going through a formal certification. These practices can be effective in terms of long-term use and initial affordability.

Effective utilization and employing current best practices in design and construction standards is a key to successful efficient building.

APPENDIX
About Professional Building Services

PBS Companies is a group of professional construction companies centered around Professional Building Services (PBS), which is an award-winning design/build firm specializing in the design, construction and renovation of buildings, including religious facilities, throughout Illinois, Northwest Indiana and Eastern Wisconsin. PBS specializes in planning for success through their Five-Step Delivery Process; by partnering with our clients, suppliers, and subcontractors to form integrated and efficient design/build teams. The product of this partnership is high-quality facilities that meet the needs and budgets of their customers.

The PBS Church Visioning Group is part of Professional Building Services, and serves the Christian church by planning, designing and building compelling worship and educational facilities that fulfill the church's ministry vision. PBS's team of professionals will strive to provide an exceptional experience incorporating practical Biblical principle application. Their goal is leadership of the construction process.

PBS Companies

Professional Building Services with an emphasis in planning, design, renovation and construction of commercial and industrial spaces.

855.672.4010
www.pbsdesignbuild.com

APPENDIX
About The Authors

Faith Building has been a culmination of the experiences of the PBS Design and Project Development Staff led by:

Dale Reiser, CCC

Dale is a graduate of Indiana University with a degree in Business Management. Dale founded Professional Building Services, Inc. in 1990. For nearly three decades, he has served in leadership in the Local Church as Elder, Adult Bible School Teacher, and Christian School Board member.

Dale has served in his local School District as Business Education Board Member and mentor. He has served on the Executive Committee and Chairman of Ignite Church Planting, President of the National Association of Church Design Builders (NACDB) Advisory Board to Chief and Wick Buildings.

Dale has traveled with missionary teams and been involved with the design and construction of ministry facilities since the 1980's.

Dale has been married to Maureen, his college sweetheart, for forty years. He is the father of three happily married adult Christians, and grandfather of four. His son, Bryan, and son-in-law, Chad are also involved in the leadership of PBS. Dale enjoys travel, boating and most winter and summer outdoor activities. As of this writing he has been blessed to be leading the PBS Design/Build, team now in its' twenty fifth year.

APPENDIX
About The Authors

PBS Catalyst, Mentor and Friend:

Ronald A. McKenzie, Architect, NCARB

Ron has been the catalyst to encourage the compilation of experiences and writing of this book. Ron is a graduate of California Polytechnic State University (Cal Poly), in 1972. He became licensed to practice architecture in California in 1978, and is a NCARB member allowing multi-state reciprocity.

In the past, he spent over twenty-five years as a consultant and is now president of President of COMPASS Consultants Corporation, a strategic business planning consultant, speaking at national conventions and seminars with clients coast-to-coast.

www.ingramcontent.com/pod-product-compliance
Lightning Source LLC
Chambersburg PA
CBHW071117210326
41519CB00020B/6330